Thoughts to Inspire & Celebrate

# MOTHER TERESA

## GLENNA HAMMER MOULTHROP

**JAICO PUBLISHING HOUSE**
Mumbai • Delhi • Bangalore • Kolkata
Hyderabad • Chennai • Ahmedabad • Bhopal

Published by Jaico Publishing House
121 Mahatma Gandhi Road
Mumbai - 400 023
jaicopub@vsnl.com
www.jaicobooks.com

Published in arrangement with:
Frederick Fell Publishers, Inc.
2131 Hollywood Boulevard, Hollywood, Florida 33020-6750.

MOTHER TERESA
ISBN 81-7992-169-7

First Jaico Impression: 2003
Third Jaico Impression: 2006

Printed by Rashmi Graphics
31, New Islam Mills Compound, Currey Road (E)
Mumbai - 400 012 • E-mail: tiwarijp@vsnl.net

*To my teacher, whose loving spirit grows in me and speaks to me, especially in the silences*

# CONTENTS

# ILLUSTRATIONS

*God writes through us, and
however imperfect
instruments we may be,
He writes beautifully.*

— *Mother Teresa*

# ACKNOWLEDGMENTS

God not only writes through us, He provides whatever we need to accomplish His work. I'd like to thank the Great Mysterious One for giving me the opportunity and means to do this book, particularly just the right people to guide and help me in many loving ways. I'm very grateful for:

Mama and Papa, Genie and Glen Hammer, who were the first ones to teach me how good it feels to be loved and to love and do for others;

my beautiful daughters Sarah and Emily, who offer me new lessons in love, joy, patience, and humility every day;

loving sisters Cindie Beaty and Marilyn Strankman, and wonderful nephews, Donald, Zachary, and Elliott, who are my heart's delight;

former bosses Jim Gallagher and LaMar Trego, who eased me gently into a new life, one that took me into Washington, D.C., and led me to "Gift of Peace," the Missionaries of Charity's hospice there;

colleague Jonathon Finley, for finding "Gift of Peace";

Sister Pietra, who opened her heart and "Gift of Peace" to me, and then held me in her prayers;

dear friend and "research assistant" Dotty Nolan, who shares my deep admiration for Mother Teresa, and always gives me new articles and books about her, as do Becky Rupp and Ghislaine Guignon;

capable friends-turned-literary-assistants Kathy Kilbury, Laurie Beitel, Bill Jacobi, Ron Hart, and the Rev. Dr. Jim Dyson, who each reviewed the first draft and provided excellent comments;

many other caring friends, especially Steve Muller, who often asked about this project and offered new ideas and encouraging words — usually when they were needed most;

and finally, Mike Towle of TowleHouse Publishing, for believing that we all need more of Mother Teresa's wisdom just as we need more of her kind of love.

**MISSIONARIES of CHARITY**
**54 A, A.J.C. BOSE ROAD**
**CALCUTTA 700016 INDIA**

＊L.D.M.

Dear Glenna Moulthrop,

Thank you for your letter.  This
brings you my prayers for God's
blessings on all that you do, and,
also on your book 'Living in Love'.
Do all for the glory of God

Keep the joy of loving God ever
burning in your heart.
Let us pray.

GOD BLESS YOU.

la Teresa mc

# THE PALM LEAF

As Christ entered Jerusalem days before His crucifixion, He was honored by those who threw palms onto His path. Since that day — nearly two thousand years ago — the palm leaf has been a Christian symbol of triumph.

The life of Mother Teresa, matriarch of the Missionaries of Charity, who serve the poor and dying throughout the world, also symbolizes such a triumph. Her message, like Christ's, is eternal: only love — pure, unconditional, self-sacrificing love — triumphs over all things.

*My vocation is love...I will <u>be</u> love and then I will be all things.*

*—Saint Thérèse of Lisieux*

# MOTHER TERESA BIOGRAPHY

When Agnes Gonxha Bojaxhiu took her vows with the Order of Loreto in 1928, she took the name "Teresa" for her religious life. In doing so she made a sacred pact to follow her patron saint, Saint Thérèse of Lisieux, whose vocation was love. Indeed, Mother Teresa lived a life of love.

At age twelve, young Agnes already knew she wanted to be a missionary and serve others. At eighteen, she joined the Institute of the Blessed Virgin Mary (Loreto Sisters), an order known for its missionary work in India. Sister Teresa, as she was known then, trained first in Dublin and later in Darjeeling, India.

During her first eighteen years in India, Sister Teresa fulfilled her calling as a teacher and then as principal of Saint Mary's High School in Calcutta. In 1946, however, she received her "call within a call" and was divinely ordered to do God's work among the destitute and dying on the streets. Teresa was, in fact, called to living that same life of poverty.

Two years later, in 1948, she was given formal permission by the church to leave the Loreto Sisters and begin a new order. And within months, Teresa's mission of love began in the slums of Calcutta. That same year, she started her first school. By 1950, Mother Teresa had founded the Missionaries of Charity, and two years later she opened a home for the dying in Calcutta.

For nearly fifty years Mother Teresa devoted her life to serving God by serving those in great need — the unwanted ones, the abandoned, the dying, and the destitute. From such a simple beginning of one school for poor children in 1948, Mother Teresa and her Missionaries of Charity, buoyed by their faith and endless compassion, have brought hope to the needy in 120 countries.

Today, more than two years after Mother Teresa's death, her mission of love — unconditional and self-sacrificing love — continues in more than six hundred homes and centers worldwide.

# INTRODUCTION

I've always been fascinated by powerful quotations. In their brevity, there's much wisdom. And there's plenty of room for one to think about how a quotation fits with her experiences. For me, quotations are great teachers. Their power is in their simplicity.

The same is true of Mother Teresa, whose life I've studied for years. Her power came from simplicity, too — a simple life grounded in God and shored up by faith and love. Since I've long been an admirer of Mother Teresa, and of a good quotation, it was natural for me to want to blend these two compelling interests in a collection of her teachings on love. All I had to do was follow Mother's lead.

Four years ago I traded a title in the corporate world for a more simple life. When concerned friends asked me why, I told them that I wanted to "live in love." Little did I know how much I had to learn. My own story, of difficult and painful lessons, is interwoven with Mother Teresa's teachings because writing this book was my primer. Through this experience, I feel like I've passed kindergarten. I now know with certainty that, for most of us, living and growing in love will be a lifelong lesson. I hope this book helps you as you learn, too.

—Glenna Hammer Moulthrop

*I*n a word, there are three things
that last forever:
faith, hope, and love,
but the greatest of these is love.

—*1 Corinthians 13:13*

*Where there is mystery, there must be faith. Faith, you cannot change no matter how you look at it.*

—*Mother Teresa*

# I
## THE INNER VOICE

In recent years my faith has deepened as I have come to see more clearly how God reveals Himself and His purpose for our lives in strange and mysterious ways. There are no coincidences in this life — only signs from God that we are on the right path. These signs come as feelings, welling up from deep within us. If we open our hearts completely and learn to be very quiet and still, God will speak to us. Some call it "the inner voice." I've also come to appreciate how God even speaks through our mouths and through the mouths of those around us. It's no wonder the ancient people called Him "the Great Mysterious One."

My story begins on a very dreary November afternoon in 1985, when, as I recall, things just didn't feel right. It was a Saturday, and my folks had spent the day as usual — shopping and running errands. When I stopped by their house for a minute, my Papa couldn't wait to show me the new shoes he'd bought for all four grandkids he adored. That's the last time I saw him alive. Within a few hours, my healthy, robust Papa was dead. Never had I experienced such a broken heart or known such weeping.

My Papa's death was just the beginning of many painful endings that intensified my fear of leaving or being left by those I love — which I called life's "comings and goings." Over the next ten years, there would be five other deaths in my immediate family, as well as the pain of caring for several close friends as they were dying.

Through these and other unwelcome transitions in my life, including a divorce, I've learned a lot about what it's like being separated from those you love. I've learned how to ride out the emotional waves and how to find comfort. I've learned more about letting go of the cherished dreams you can lose in a heartbeat. And, most importantly, I've learned that endings are really new beginnings in disguise.

As spiritual beings, we continually die to our old ways to be reborn into a new life. As this process continues, life becomes deeper, richer, and fuller — if we grow in God and in love.

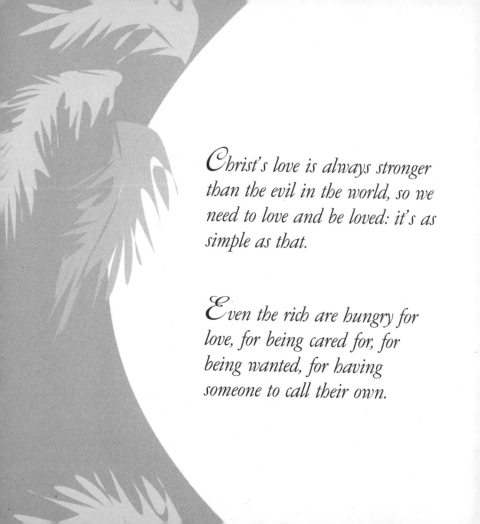

*Christ's* love is always stronger than the evil in the world, so we need to love and be loved: it's as simple as that.

*Even* the rich are hungry for love, for being cared for, for being wanted, for having someone to call their own.

*Each* of us has a mission to fulfill: a mission of love. At the hour of death, when we come face-to-face with God, we are going to be judged on love; not on how much we have done, but on how much love we have put into our actions.

*We* can do no great things, only small things with great love.

*From* the abundance of the heart, the mouth speaks. If your heart is full of love, you will speak of love.

*Love* has no meaning if it isn't shared. Love has to be put into action. You have to love without expectation, to do something for love itself, not for what you may receive.

*I*n the developed countries, there is a poverty of intimacy, a poverty of spirit, of loneliness, of lack of love. There is no greater sickness in the world today than that one.

*T*ry not to judge people. If you judge others then you are not giving love. Instead, try to help them by seeing their needs and acting to meet them.

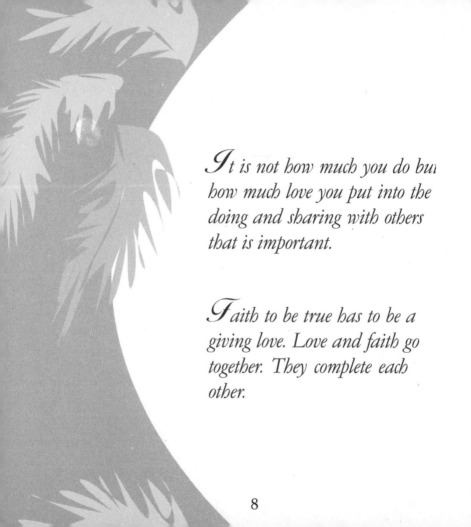

*I*t is not how much you do but how much love you put into the doing and sharing with others that is important.

*F*aith to be true has to be a giving love. Love and faith go together. They complete each other.

8

*I think God is telling us something with AIDS, giving us an opportunity to show our love. People with AIDS have awakened the tender love in those who had perhaps shut it out and forgotten it.*

*A clean heart can see God, can speak to God, and can see the love of God in others.*

9

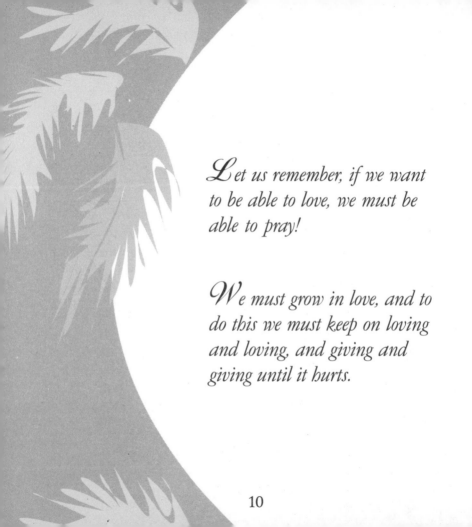

*L*et us remember, if we want to be able to love, we must be able to pray!

*W*e must grow in love, and to do this we must keep on loving and loving, and giving and giving until it hurts.

*Faithfulness to the little things will help us grow in love.*

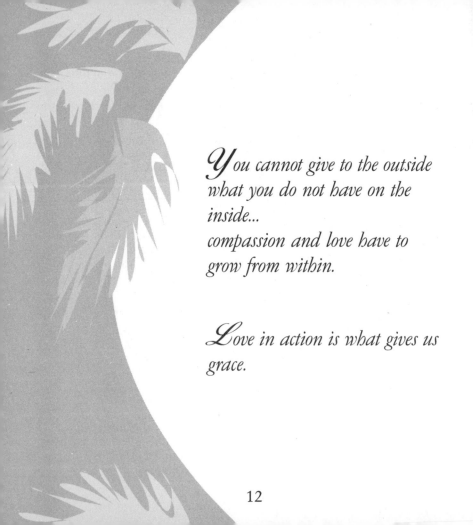

*You* cannot give to the outside what you do not have on the inside...
compassion and love have to grow from within.

*Love* in action is what gives us grace.

12

*We* can cure physical diseases with medicine, but the only cure for loneliness, despair, and hopelessness is love.

*There* are many in the world who are dying for a piece of bread, but there are many more dying for a little love.

13

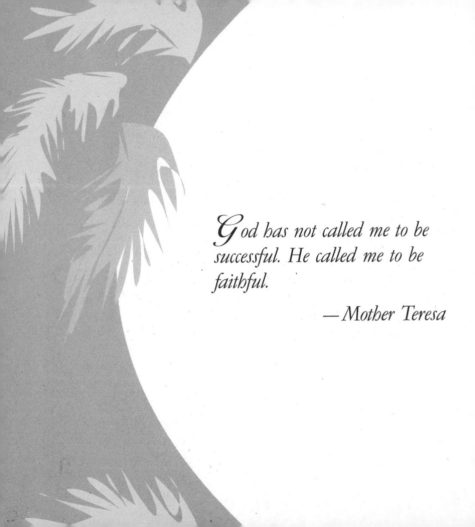

*God has not called me to be successful. He called me to be faithful.*

—*Mother Teresa*

# II
## LETTING GO AND LETTING GOD

Another profound ending came into my life in the fall of 1995. After much soul-searching, I let go of a long, well established career — a career that for many years had been very gratifying and fulfilling. It meant, of course, that I'd have to leave the people I'd come to love — my work family. But I yearned for something more, and I knew I wanted to grow in new ways.

As a manager in a tough business that was subject to constant public scrutiny and criticism, I couldn't remember a work week shorter than fifty-five or sixty hours. As a single parent, I would come home every night to even greater responsibilities. Life was passing me by; I wanted to slow it down, simplify it, and enjoy it more fully. I longed for the things of the spirit, the simple pleasures that fill me up: music, cooking, writing, quiet walks, and just having more time to be with those I love. I intended to take at least a year off to "catch my breath." God, I think, had other plans.

It was the holiday season; Mother Teresa's book *A Simple Path* had just hit the bookstores. As soon as I saw an ad for it, I knew that I had to read it. In one passage, Mother Teresa talked about the work that the Missionaries of Charity do with AIDS victims and about the first hospices they started in new York City, San Francisco, and Washington, D.C. *Washington, D.C.!* I couldn't believe it — I'd been to D.C. several times already that month, and I'd be going again that January. In an instant I knew what I was meant to do. I had to find my way to Mother Teresa's hospice — I had to see it for myself.

*If* you don't believe in God, you can help others by doing works of love, and the fruit of these works are the extra graces that come into your soul.

*Do* what you do best, but do it for the love of God, not fame or riches, and you will begin helping the whole world.

17

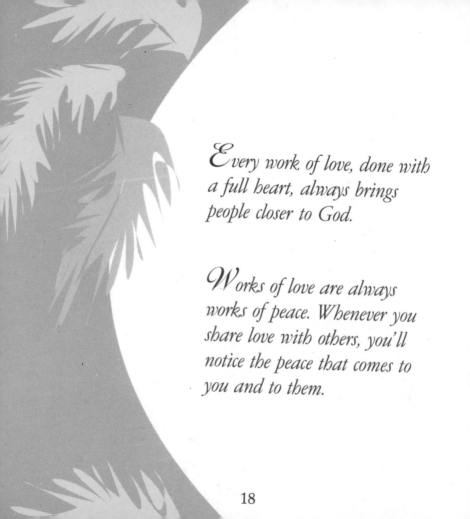

*E*very work of love, done with a full heart, always brings people closer to God.

*W*orks of love are always works of peace. Whenever you share love with others, you'll notice the peace that comes to you and to them.

18

*W*e have all been created for greater things — to love and be loved. Love is love — to love a person without any conditions, without any expectations.

*S*mall things, done in great love, bring joy and peace.

*E*ach moment is all we need,
not more. Be happy now and if
you show through your actions
that you love others, including
those who are poorer than you,
you'll give them happiness, too.

*L*ove is a fruit in season at all
times, and within reach of every
hand. Anyone may gather it
and no limit is set.

*To love, it is necessary to give. To give, it is necessary to be free from selfishness.*

*The most terrible disease that can ever strike a human being is to have no one near him to be loved. Without a heart full of love, without generous hands, it is impossible to cure a man suffering of loneliness.*

*You* must give what will cost you something...then your gift becomes a sacrifice, which will have value before God. Any sacrifice is useful if it is done out of love.

*Love* is proved by deeds; the more they cost us, the greater the proof of our love.

$\mathcal{D}$o ordinary things with extraordinary love.

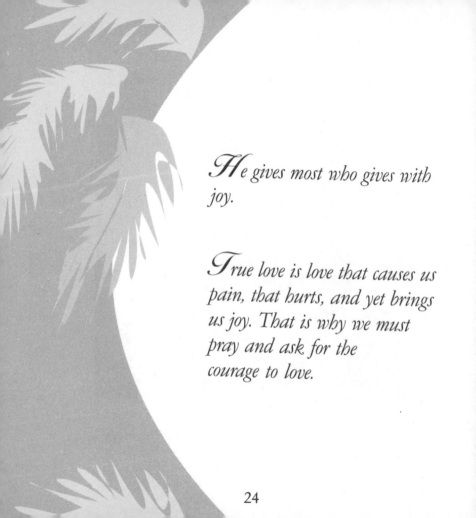

*H*e gives most who gives with joy.

*T*rue love is love that causes us pain, that hurts, and yet brings us joy. That is why we must pray and ask for the courage to love.

*Prayer begets faith, faith begets love, and love begets service.*

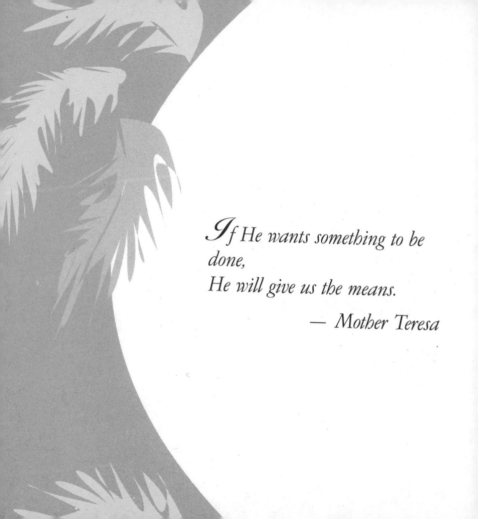

*If* He wants something to be done,
He will give us the means.

— *Mother Teresa*

# III
## THE BLESSING

After arriving in D.C., I wasted no time in calling a number that I had been given for the Missionaries of Charity. I was told, however, that I would have to call back after 9:00 P.M. and that I would need to ask for Sister Pietra.

Later that same night, I followed my instructions carefully, waiting on the line for what seemed like several minutes. Finally, a soft voice said, "Hello, I am Sister Pietra." I began to tell her my story about being a volunteer in an AIDS support group in my community and how my friends and I had helped raise money for a new hospice house where I live. I told her that I had traveled a long way and that I was in D.C. on business. I told her how much I wanted to come and work at their hospice on Saturday.

In a kind way, Sister Pietra said that wasn't possible — that no one is allowed to work there unless they have been through special training. "When will you be back?" she asked. "We will be giving another orientation in April." I explained to Sister Pietra that I really didn't know when my work would bring me back to D.C., that I was here now, and I had planned my trip so that I could stay over that Saturday. Again, she said kindly but firmly, "You don't understand. I may not even be here this Saturday. It is impossible."

A bit taken aback, I took a deep breath and began speaking in words I didn't recognize. "No, Sister. You do not understand. I need to come because it will bless me. I need the blessing." And then I began to pour out from my heart the rest of my story. I told her about my precious nephew, the one who had always been like my own child — about his life on the streets and how he had contracted AIDS by the time he was twenty-two. As Sister Pietra listened quietly, I told her about how his father, my only brother, had died when this beloved child was just two and how estranged my nephew and his mother were throughout his life. And I told her that, in spite of great fears, my mother and my sisters and I had brought him home and cared for him those last weeks he lived because he longed to be with us. I also shared with her that I had never known such peace and joy and love, and that in spite of this being such a sad time in my life, I felt incredibly blessed by it, too.

"So, you see, Sister," I said through my tears, "I need to do this. It will bless me." And, without hesitation, she answered, "Be here at 9:00 A.M. Saturday and ask for me."

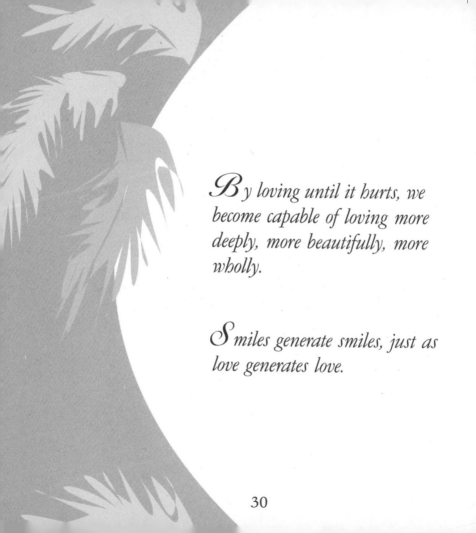

*By* loving until it hurts, we become capable of loving more deeply, more beautifully, more wholly.

*Smiles* generate smiles, just as love generates love.

*We don't need to look for happiness: If we have love for others, we'll be given it. It is the gift of God.*

*The world never needed love more than today: people are starving for love.*

*Joy is a net of love by which you can catch souls.*

*You cannot love two people perfectly, but you can love all people perfectly if you love the one Jesus in them all. This means that one should center mind and heart, life, and activity on Jesus, seeing Him in every human sufferer.*

*Love always unites. It does not divide.*

*H*oliness is to love God and love people. It is therefore not a luxury reserved for a favored few. All are invited to be holy.

*W*e have to pour our love on someone. And people are the means of expressing our love for God.

*Let us all keep the joy of loving God in our hearts, and share this joy of loving one another as He loves each one of us.*

*Good works are links forming a chain of love around the world.*

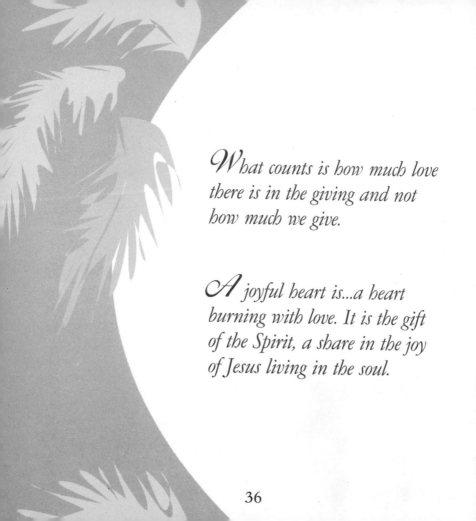

*What* counts is how much love
there is in the giving and not
how much we give.

*A* joyful heart is...a heart
burning with love. It is the gift
of the Spirit, a share in the joy
of Jesus living in the soul.

*There is no great difference in the reality of one country or another because it is always people you meet everywhere. They may look different or be dressed differently or may have a different education or position. But they are all the same. They are all people to be loved.*

37

*Everybody has something good inside. Some hide it, some neglect it, but it is there.*

—Mother Teresa

# IV
## GIFT OF PEACE

Waiting for a taxi early that Saturday, I remembered the concerns that some colleagues had for my safety. Some doubted whether I'd even be able to get a taxi back downtown once I got out to the hospice. I felt uneasy. The taxi driver made matters worse. Not only was he uncertain about the address I gave him, there was no way he would promise to return for me.

As the taxi took me away, I sat quietly in the back, wondering what was next. When we had driven for some time, the taxi driver began to ask me questions about "this place, Gift of Peace." I tried my best to explain about Mother Teresa and the Missionaries of Charity, about their work among the poor and dying around the world — and even here in D.C. He continued to ask me questions, and with each one, I could hear his voice soften. By the time we arrived at the hospice, he turned to me and said, "You go to the door, and I'll wait to make sure someone answers." When the door opened, I went back to the taxi to pay my fare. Then, in a caring voice, he said, "I really can't promise you anything, but if there's any way that I can be back here at noon to pick you up, I will."

In a fifteen-minute taxi ride, somewhere through the outlying neighborhoods of Washington, D.C. — far from the security of my hotel — I had witnessed a transformation. God, whose love and power is infinite and absolute, had worked in His wonderfully mysterious way. Before my very eyes, He softened the heart of this stranger I had hired to take me safely to Mother Teresa's "Gift of Peace," her spartan hospice on N.E. Otis Street.

*Love is giving the best we have.*

*L*ove starts at home and lasts at home ...the home is each person's first field of loving, devotion, and service.

*I*t is easy to love people far away. It is easier to give a cup of rice than to relieve the loneliness and pain of someone unloved in our own home.

*We* all should become carriers
of God's love. But to do this, we
must deepen our life of love and
prayer and sacrifice.

*When* you know how much
God is in love with you, then
you can only live your life
radiating that love.

*L*ove begins in the family.
Peace begins in the family.
Where there is love, there is
unity, peace, and joy.

*Y*our suffering is a great
means of love, if you make use
of it, especially if you offer it for
peace in the world.

*I think the world today is upside down. It is suffering so much because there is so little love in the home and in family life. We have no time for our children. We have no time for each other.*

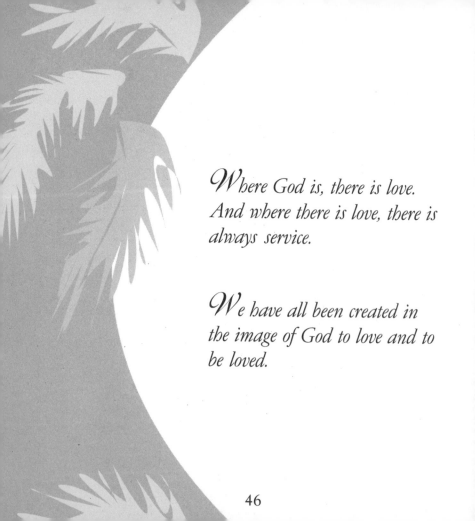

*Where God is, there is love. And where there is love, there is always service.*

*We have all been created in the image of God to love and to be loved.*

*In the silence of the heart,
God speaks and you have to
listen. Then in the fullness of
your heart, because it is full of
God, full of love, full of
compassion, full of faith, your
mouth will speak.*

*Love has no other message but
its own.*

*Pain, sorrow, feelings of loneliness are nothing but the kiss of Jesus, a sign that you have come so close that He can kiss you.*

—*Mother Teresa*

# V

## IN THE PRESENCE
## OF ANGELS

Once I was inside the hospice, any doubt that I had experienced vanished quickly. I was awed by two things: the stark simplicity of the hospice and the radiance of the sisters, clad in their flowing white saris. The contentment and peace on their faces was undeniable. I knew that I was in the presence of angels, for sure — these loving sisters bound, with Mother Teresa, to God in serving others.

When Sister Pietra came to greet me, she quickly took me to one of the other sisters for my work assignment. Although I had longed to care for AIDS patients, I was assigned to help with the morning baths and grooming of the elderly. For the next three hours, the sisters bathed individuals, partially dressed them, and then brought them to me, one-by-one, to powder them, to comb their hair, to clip their nails — to simply care for them, to be loving with them. Time passed quickly.

Soon, Sister Pietra reappeared. After thanking me for helping out, she pointed down the long basement hallway to a set of doors. "That is the way," she said. As I approached the doors, a sign posted on one caught my attention. It was a scripture from Psalms: "The Lord shall watch over your going out and your coming in from this time forth, forevermore." Without a voice, in the quiet of that dark hallway, God had surely spoken to me and I heard it.

Here I was, almost forty-eight years old — on the outside a woman others had described as strong-willed, decisive, capable. For as long as I could re-member, I had been fiercely independent and quite proud of it. But on the inside was this sorrowful little girl who couldn't bear the thought of being separated from one more person she loved — all of the "comings and goings" of life had been far more pain-ful than she could admit, even to herself.

*O*ur life of contemplation,
simply put, is to realize God's
constant presence and His
tender love for us in the least
little things of life.

*I*f we pray, our hearts become
clean, and we are filled with
the love of God — a love that
gives without counting the cost;
love that is tender and
compassionate; love that forgives.

51

*I*f I forgive then I can be holy and can pray. All this comes from a humble heart, and if we have this, we will know how to love God, to love self, and to love neighbor.

*B*e kind to each other: It is better to commit faults with gentleness than to work miracles with unkindness.

*G*od loves us with a tender
love. That is all that Jesus came
to teach us: the tender love of
God.

*P*ray lovingly like children,
with an earnest desire to love
much and to make loved the
one that is not loved.

*Loving must be as normal to us as living and breathing, day after day, until our death.*

*When you feel lonely, when you feel unwanted, when you feel sick and forgotten, remember you are precious to God. He loves you. Show that love for one another.*

*It* is a wonderful thing that
God Himself loves me tenderly.
That is why we should have
courage, joy, and the conviction
that nothing can separate us
from the love of Christ.

*It* is the intensity of love we
put into our gestures that makes
them into something beautiful
for God.

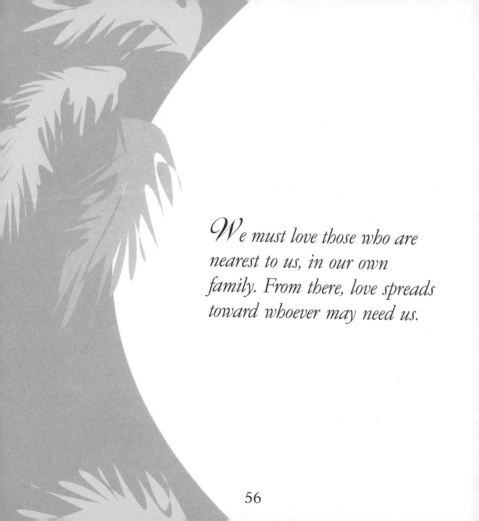

*We must love those who are nearest to us, in our own family. From there, love spreads toward whoever may need us.*

*The fruit of faith is love.*

*I want you to go and find the poor in your own homes. Above all, your love has to start there.*

*Let us all be one heart, full of love.*

*When we all see God in each other, we will love one another as He loves us all.*

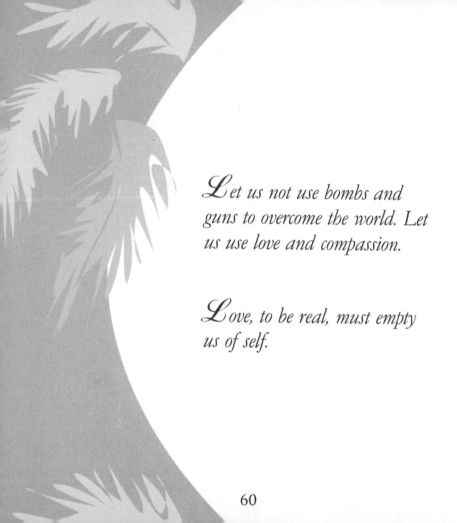

*Let* us not use bombs and guns to overcome the world. Let us use love and compassion.

*Love*, to be real, must empty us of self.

60

*There are Danish children who make sacrifices in order to be able to offer others a glass of milk every day. And German children do the same...these are concrete ways of teaching love. When these children grow up, they will know what it means to give.*

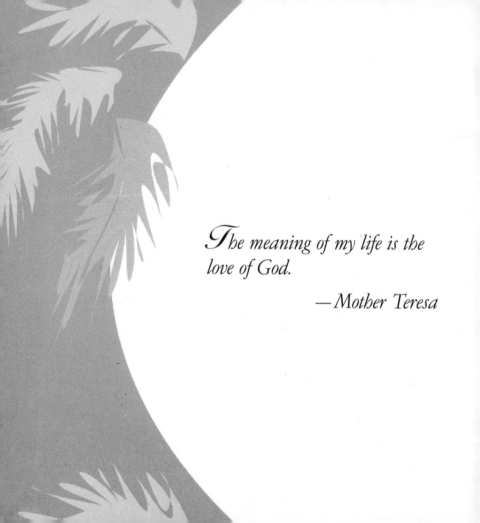

*The meaning of my life is the love of God.*

*— Mother Teresa*

# VI
## AN ENDLESS LOVE

Why did God lead me to that hospice, far away in Washington, D.C.? And why to Mother Teresa?

Perhaps it's because I longed for constancy. Clearly, Mother Teresa lived with more constancy than most of us. She lived in love — from a heart fully aware that she was doing exactly what God intended for her to do. When we live as she did — perfectly centered in our purpose and using the special gifts that God gives each of us to love and serve others — we are given "the gift of peace." And, God fills us with His love. In a world where nothing seems to last, where there are always "comings and goings" and much uncertainty, we are never really alone. God is always in us. We are never separated from Him or

His love.

To this day I'm still growing in my understanding of that experience on N.E. Otis Street. Without realizing it, I'd been on a spiritual journey for a very long time. Every death and separation had been a painful part of that journey. I'd been dying to the old "realities" only to be reborn into a deeper, richer, fuller understanding of myself and of the God who lives in me, who is with me always and whose love is endless. I'd been learning to live in love.

That is my wish for you. May you also know that the Great Mysterious One — whose love and power triumphs over all things, is absolute and never ending — watches over your "going out and your coming in," too.

*Give of your hands to serve and your hearts to love.*

*What matters is the gift of yourself, the degree of love you put into each one of your actions.*

*L*et us not be satisfied with just paying money. Money is not enough. Money can be got. The poor need your hands to serve them. They need your heart to love them.

*I*n order for us to be able to love, we need to have faith because faith is love in action, and love in action is service.

*B*e an angel of comfort to the
sick, a friend to the little ones,
and love each other as God
loves each one of you with a
special, most intense love.

*L*ove, an abundant love, is the
expression of our Christian
religion.

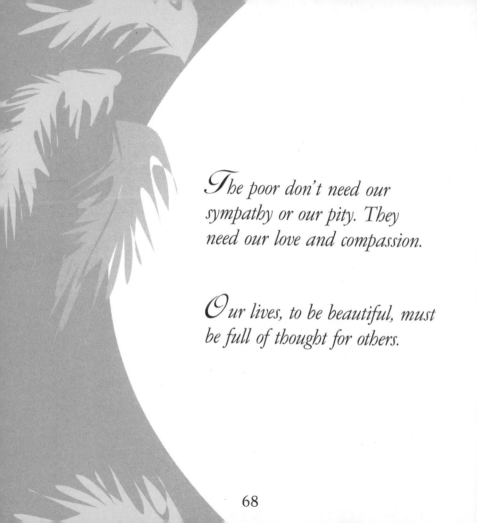

*The* poor don't need our sympathy or our pity. They need our love and compassion.

*Our* lives, to be beautiful, must be full of thought for others.

*I*t is a gift of God to be able to share our love
with others.

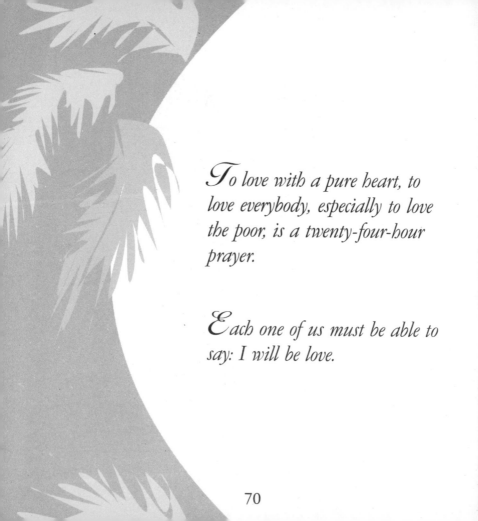

*To* love with a pure heart, to love everybody, especially to love the poor, is a twenty-four-hour prayer.

*Each* one of us must be able to say: I will be love.

70

*Let us interweave our lives
with bonds of sacrifice and love,
and it will be possible for us to
conquer the world.*

*The world is lost for want of
sweetness and kindness.*

*T*hose of you who are sick, when things are hard, take refuge in Christ's heart. There, my own heart will find you with strength and love.

*G*od's love for us is greater than all the conflicts, which shall pass.

*Every child is a sign of God's love.*

*You call Him Ishwar, some call him Allah, some simply God. But we all have to acknowledge that it is He who made us for greater things: to love and be loved.*

# BIBLIOGRAPHY

Bartos, Pat. "Someone Beautiful Goes to God." *Our Sunday Visitor,* September 21, 1997 (Vol. 86, No. 21), pp. 2-23.

Beneate, Becky and Joseph Duprepos, editors. *No Greater Love.* Novato, Calif.: New World Library, 1997, pp. 4, 9, 13-16, 20-24, 26-30, 32, 38, 42, 58, 98, 125, 128-129, 136, 137, 179.

Beneate, Becky, editor. *In the Heart of the World.* Novato, Calif.: New World Library, 1997, pp. 13, 29, 40, 42, 45, 60, 107.

Commemorative Program, Père Marquette Discovery Award, presented to Mother Teresa at Marquette University, June 1981.

Doig, Desmond. *Mother Teresa, Her People and Her Work.* New York: Harper & Row, 1976, p. 162.

Egan, Eileen. *Such a Vision of the Street: Mother Teresa, the Spirit and the Work.* Garden City, N.Y.: Doubleday, 1985, pp. 220, 324, 341, 357.

Gonzalez-Balado, Jose Luis, and Janet N. Playfoot, editors. *My Life for the Poor: Mother Teresa of Calcutta.* San Francisco:

Harper & Row, 1985, pp. 33, 37, 44, 57, 72, 73, 100, 104.

LaPierre, Dominique. *Compassion; Mother Teresa Persists with Love.* New York Times News Service, December 25, 1994.

LeJoly, Edward. *Mother Teresa of Calcutta: A Biography.* San Francisco: Harper & Row, 1985, pp. 161, 177, 179, 180, 185, 211, 255.

Mother Teresa, "Letter to Friends of the Missionaries of Charity," March 12, 1996.

Muggeridge, Malcolm. *Something Beautiful for God; Mother Teresa of Calcutta.* New York: Harper & Row, 1971, pp. 65, 72, 73, 98, 112.

Prince Michael of Greece. "All the Lives We Touch," *Parade,* August 11, 1996, pp. 4-5.

Rai, Raghu, and Navin Chawala, *The Life and Work of Mother Teresa.* Rockport, Mass.: Element Books, 1996, pp. 90, 158, 191, 192.

Shelton, Karen Eberhardt. "The Woman Who Loved the World," *Family Circle,* February 17, 1998, p. 154.

Vardey, Lucinda, compiler, *Mother Teresa: A Simple Path,* New York: Ballantine Books, 1995, pp. 7-8, 40, 43, 52, 80-81, 87, 93, 99, 101, 108, 171, 181.

# THE AUTHOR

Glenna Hammer Moulthrop, a former communications executive with Westinghouse, owns a consulting business in government and public affairs and fundraising. During a twenty-five-year career in communications and newspaper reporting, Moulthrop won dozens of writing and editing awards. However, it was her very first award — earned as a third-grader — for a review of "The Story of Jesus" that still means the most to her. As an eight-year-old reviewing the book, she simply wrote, "It made me feel good inside."

Moulthrop lives with her two college-age daughters in the Tri-Cities of Washington, where she also serves on the board of several community organizations. It is the Tri-Cities Chaplaincy Hospice House and Counseling Center, however, that has her heart. She organizes the center's two largest fundraisers each year and assists in many programs that help the troubled, the dying, and those struggling with HIV/AIDS.